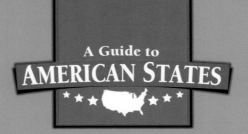

A Guide to
AMERICAN STATES

West Virginia

THE MOUNTAIN STATE

www.av2books.com

AV² provides enriched content that supplements and complements this book. Weigl's AV² books strive to create inspired learning and engage young minds in a total learning experience.

Your AV² Media Enhanced books come alive with...

Audio
Listen to sections of the book read aloud.

Key Words
Study vocabulary, and complete a matching word activity.

Video
Watch informative video clips.

Quizzes
Test your knowledge.

Go to **www.av2books.com**, and enter this book's unique code.

Embedded Weblinks
Gain additional information for research.

Slide Show
View images and captions, and prepare a presentation.

BOOK CODE

C 1 2 5 7 4 4

Try This!
Complete activities and hands-on experiments.

... and much, much more!

AV² by Weigl brings you media enhanced books that support active learning.

Published by AV² by Weigl
350 5th Avenue, 59th Floor
New York, NY 10118
Website: www.av2books.com   www.weigl.com

Library of Congress Cataloging-in-Publication Data

Lawton, Val.
 West Virginia / Val Lawton.
    p. cm. -- (A guide to American states)
 Includes index.
 ISBN 978-1-61690-822-5 (hardcover : alk. paper) -- ISBN 978-1-61690-497-5 (online)
 1. West Virginia--Juvenile literature. I. Title.
 F241.3.L393 2011
 975.4--dc23
                        2011019238

Printed in the United States of America in North Mankato, Minnesota

052011
WEP180511

Project Coordinator Jordan McGill
Art Director Terry Paulhus

Photo Credits
Every reasonable effort has been made to trace ownership and to obtain permission to reprint copyright material. The publishers would be pleased to have any errors or omissions brought to their attention so that they may be corrected in subsequent printings.

Weigl acknowledges Getty Images as its primary image supplier for this title.

Contents

Harpers Ferry is a historic town in Jefferson County. It is located where the Potomac and Shenandoah rivers meet.

Introduction

West Virginia justifies in every way its nickname, the Mountain State. With an average altitude of 1,500 feet above sea level, it is the highest of any U.S. state east of the Mississippi River. It boasts spectacular scenery, beautiful farms, and misty rolling hills. West Virginia also has a rich history and culture that makes visiting the state a rewarding and memorable experience.

West Virginia separated from the state of Virginia during the Civil War. A series of disagreements between the eastern and western parts of Virginia caused the separation. The people of western Virginia felt unfairly taxed and believed that they were receiving few benefits. In addition, many West Virginians were opposed to slave-owning, while wealthy eastern planters had many slaves.

West Virginia is famous for its rolling hills and mountains. Three-fourths of the state is covered in forests.

West Virginia usually ranks among the top 10 states in apple production.

The capital of West Virginia is Charleston. It is located in Kanawha County, where the Elk and the Kanawha rivers meet. When Charleston was established in 1794, the total population was 35. It is now the largest city in the state, with a population of more than 50,000 people. Charleston is referred to as both the "most northern" of Southern cities and the "most southern" of Northern cities in the United States. The city has many historic buildings and grand mansions. Many of these landmarks date back to the late 1800s. Downtown Charleston draws many tourists with its entertainment, shops, and trolley-bus rides.

Like all of the other large West Virginia cities, Charleston is located in a river valley, where the land is flat. West Virginia's other major cities are Huntington, Wheeling, Parkersburg, and Morgantown.

Where Is West Virginia?

Located in the middle of the Appalachian Mountains, West Virginia is the most mountainous state east of the Rocky Mountains. The state's unusual boundaries, created by mountains and rivers, give it the shape of a pan with two large handles. This shape inspired one of West Virginia's nicknames, the Panhandle State.

Autumn in West Virginia is beautiful as forest-covered hillsides begin to turn shades of red and yellow.

West Virginia is known for its unique **rural** mountain culture. Since their mountain location was quite isolated, early West Virginians developed a local culture that was not influenced by neighboring populations. Many of these mountain traditions, such as folk songs and storytelling, still exist today.

Drivers in West Virginia take advantage of the more than 37,370 miles of roads that cross the state. About 550 miles of these roads are interstate highways. For those who prefer to fly, Yeager Airport, near Charleston, is West Virginia's main airport. A railroad takes passengers through Charleston and the southern part of the state.

I DIDN'T KNOW THAT!

West Virginia is divided into 55 counties.

West Virginia is a small state, covering about 24,000 square miles of land. Forty other states are larger than West Virginia.

Illinois and South Carolina also have cities named Charleston.

Amtrak operates two daily long-distance trains and 10 stations in West Virginia.

Mapping West Virginia

West Virginia is bordered by Pennsylvania and Maryland to the north. Virginia is to the east and the south. Kentucky and Ohio are to the west. The Ohio River forms the border between Ohio and West Virginia. The Potomac River forms part of West Virginia's northern border with Maryland. The Potomac then flows southeast past Washington, D.C., and into Chesapeake Bay.

Sites and Symbols

STATE SEAL
West Virginia

STATE BIRD
Northern Cardinal

STATE FLOWER
Rhododendron

STATE FLAG
West Virginia

STATE ANIMAL
Black Bear

STATE TREE
Sugar Maple

Nickname The Mountain State

Motto *Montani Semper Liberi*
(Mountaineers Are Always Free)

Song "This Is My West Virginia," words and music by Iris Bell, "West Virginia, My Home Sweet Home," words and music by Julian G. Hearne, Jr., "The West Virginia Hills," words by David King and music by H. E. Engle

Entered the Union June 20, 1863, as the 35th state

Capital Charleston

Population (2010 Census) 1,852,994 Ranked 37th state

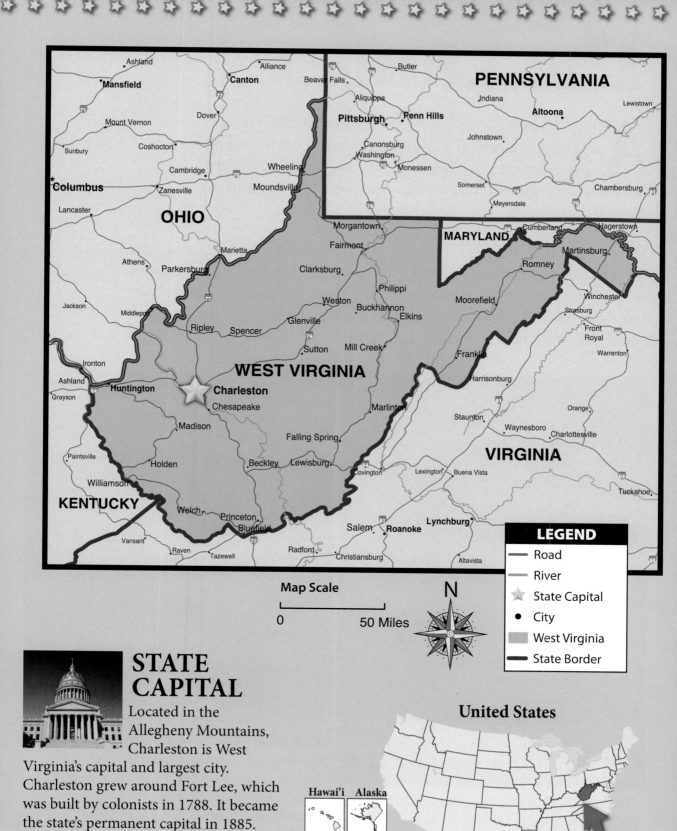

STATE CAPITAL

Located in the Allegheny Mountains, Charleston is West Virginia's capital and largest city. Charleston grew around Fort Lee, which was built by colonists in 1788. It became the state's permanent capital in 1885.

United States

West Virginia

The Land

All of West Virginia lies within the geographic region known as the Appalachian Mountain System. This region extends from Canada to Alabama. The state is further divided into two separate regions. They are the Allegheny Plateau and the Appalachian Ridge.

The Appalachian Ridge is made up of long mountain ridges, which are covered in forests. The Blue Ridge Mountains form the eastern edge of the Appalachian Ridge and are visible from the Eastern Panhandle. The Allegheny Plateau stretches from the Mohawk Valley in New York to the Cumberland Plateau in southern West Virginia.

SENECA ROCKS

The Seneca Rocks formation rises nearly 900 feet above the North Fork River. It is one of West Virginia's most visited natural sites.

APPALACHIAN MOUNTAINS

The Appalachian Mountains are thought to be among the oldest mountains in the world. This mountain system extends almost 2,000 miles from Labrador and New Brunswick in Canada southwest to Alabama.

NEW RIVER

The New River, anything but new, has been flowing for more than 300 million years. Geologists believe that it is the oldest river in North America. The Grandview Overlook offers a spectacular view of this waterway.

BLACKWATER FALLS

Blackwater Falls State Park features a spectacular waterfall that drops almost 60 feet. This waterfall got its name because acid in the water gives it a dark color. The acid comes from tree needles that have fallen into the water.

Bluestone Lake is the endpoint of the 11-mile-long Bluestone National Scenic River. It is a popular tourist destination.

Harpers Ferry is the lowest point of land in West Virginia. It is 280 feet above sea level.

The highest point in the state is Spruce Knob. It rises 4,861 feet above sea level.

West Virginia is known for its thick, rolling fog, which occurs around its many rivers and high mountain ranges.

Climate

Much of West Virginia lies on the Allegheny Plateau. At the highest point of the plateau, the weather is severe and can change suddenly. Dense fogs can collect, and fierce winds often blow. West Virginia is often humid.

Average January temperatures in West Virginia range from 28° Fahrenheit to 38° F. Average July temperatures vary from 68° F to 76° F. Average annual temperatures range from 56° F in the southwest to 48° F in more mountainous areas with a higher elevation.

Average Annual Precipitation Across West Virginia

Alderson, Charleston, and Parkersburg receive less than 45 inches of rain per year. Other areas in the state, such as Pickens, receive more than 65 inches of rainfall per year. What aspects of Pickens' location within the state make it so much wetter than other areas?

Inches of Rainfall

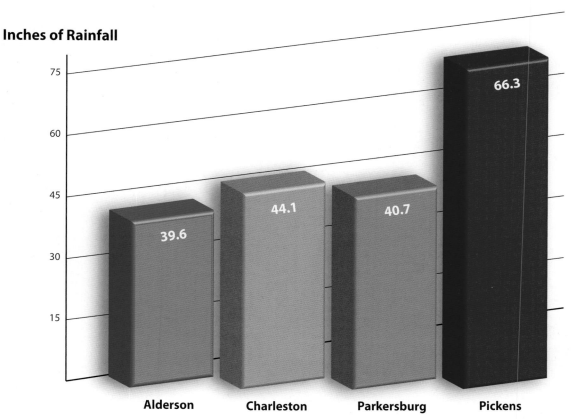

Natural Resources

West Virginia has many natural resources. It is among the nation's leading sources of **bituminous coal**, producing more than 140 million tons per year. Stone, cement, salt, and oil are also important resources for the state.

Barges transport millions of tons of coal and other cargo on the Kanawha River every year.

The oil and gas industry in West Virginia is linked to the salt industry. In the early 1800s, oil and gas were of little importance. Salt workers in the Kanawha Valley often struck oil or gas while drilling for salt. They thought it was a nuisance. Once the value of oil and natural gas as fuels was recognized, petroleum and gas production in the region boomed. For many years, West Virginia was the largest producer of natural gas east of the Mississippi River. The state still produces large amounts of natural gas in the Appalachian Basin.

Today West Virginia companies are drilling for natural gas. They hope to find deposits that may hold trillions of cubic feet of this fuel.

I DIDN'T KNOW THAT!

Over the years more than 1.5 million acres of West Virginia have been affected by coal mining. The state's Office of Abandoned Mine Lands and Reclamation is in charge of restoring these polluted areas to their natural state.

Ginseng, a plant that grows naturally in West Virginia's cool, moist forests, has been harvested there for more than 200 years. Ginseng root is used as a spice, as a natural medicine, and as the basis for tea.

A 34-carat diamond was uncovered in 1928 at Peterstown. No other diamonds have been found since.

West Virginia is ranked the third-most-forested state in the nation, behind Maine and New Hampshire. Many of its trees are used for lumber.

Plants

Compared to mountain ranges in the western United States, the Appalachians have deep soil in which many plants flourish. In Kanawha State Forest, visitors can find a wide variety of trees and plants. They include 23 species of wild orchids. West Virginia is the habitat of many flowering bushes, such as laurel, hepatica, wild geranium, and black-eyed Susan. Oak, maple, birch, and pine trees all grow in West Virginia.

Another region that stands out for its fertile soil and fine climate is the valley of the New River. Over millions of years, the New River has moved many tons of rich **sediment** into its lower valley. As a result, the soil along the valley floor is ideal for growing plants and produces an abundant amount of lush vegetation.

OAK TREE

Oak trees lose their leaves each winter. Smaller oak trees usually grow 20 to 30 feet tall, and large ones can be as tall as 100 feet tall.

MAPLE TREE

West Virginia made the sugar maple its official state tree in 1949. Sugar maples provide valuable timber and maple syrup.

SUNFLOWERS

About 18 kinds of sunflowers grow in West Virginia. The plants may grow several feet high.

SOAPWORT

Soapwort is a plant common in the summer. The flowers are pink or white. The leaves froth like soap when they are crushed.

Pine trees are called evergreens, because they do not lose their leaves during the winter.

The great laurel, or rhododendron, was made the official state flower of West Virginia in 1903.

Animals

I n the area around Bluestone State Park, blue herons, kingfishers, bobcats, foxes, and wild turkeys can be seen in the woods. Many kinds of large mammals have disappeared from the state, but deer and black bears can still be found in the high country. Trout, bass, and pike swim in West Virginia's streams and rivers.

West Virginia has many different kinds of birds. Loons, ducks, and geese are **migratory** species. Quails, woodcocks, owls, eagles, and hawks also fly in West Virginia's skies. The songs of the cardinal, wood thrush, brown thrasher, and scarlet tanager can be heard throughout the state.

NORTHERN CARDINAL

The cardinal was made West Virginia's official state bird in 1949. The males are deep red with black masks. Cardinals are small, measuring about 8 inches.

OPOSSUM

Opossums are found across West Virginia. Excellent tree climbers, they can use their tail as a fifth limb. These scavengers eat whatever is around.

BROOK TROUT

The brook trout has been West Virginia's official state fish since 1973. The brook trout thrives in cool, spring-fed streams and lakes. It cannot survive in warmer water.

TIMBER RATTLESNAKE

Timber rattlesnakes are present across most of the United States. They live in the high woods and rugged mountains of West Virginia. These **venomous** snakes will not pursue or attack a person unless threatened or provoked.

A few decades ago, black bear sightings in West Virginia were rare. Because of efforts to protect bears and the areas in which they live, their numbers have increased.

The monarch butterfly has been West Virginia's official state butterfly since 1995. Monarchs are most often found near fields and waterways.

The Cheat Mountain salamander and the flat-spired three-toothed land snail live only in West Virginia.

Tourism

Tourism is very important to West Virginia's economy. The state's natural beauty attracts visitors from across the country. There are plenty of outdoor activities to enjoy in West Virginia's nine state forests and 35 state parks, including fishing, hunting, river rafting, hiking, camping, and skiing. More than a million acres of West Virginia land are dedicated to parks.

Mineral springs are another popular attraction found throughout the state. The best known are those at Berkeley Springs and White Sulphur Springs. Berkeley Springs is the oldest **spa** in the country.

NEW RIVER GORGE BRIDGE

The New River Gorge Bridge is the country's longest single-arch steel bridge. It is 3,030 feet long.

BECKLEY EXHIBITION COAL MINE

Visitors to the Beckley Exhibition Coal Mine can explore some of the 1,500 feet of underground passages, ride in an underground coal car, and experience what the lives of West Virginia's rugged miners might have been like in the early 1900s.

CASS SCENIC RAILROAD STATE PARK

Cass Scenic Railroad State Park is located in Pocahontas County. The heritage railroad with its steam-driven locomotives stretches 11 miles.

CANAAN VALLEY

Canaan Valley is considered to have some of the best skiing in the mid-Atlantic states. The valley has six resorts to accommodate skiers. Snow in the valley often lasts well into the spring.

President George Washington and his wife, Martha, often visited Berkeley Springs.

Jefferson Rock in the Shenandoah Valley was named for Thomas Jefferson, who helped survey the area as a young man.

Harpers Ferry is the site of **abolitionist** John Brown's famous raid on a U.S. arsenal and armory. The armory was one of the main suppliers of rifles in both the War of 1812 and the Civil War. The John Brown Wax Museum tells the story of Brown and his hanging.

The Monongahela National Forest was established in 1920. About 1.3 million visitors come to the national forest each year to hike, backpack, hunt, and fish.

Visitors to West Virginia spend more than $4 billion per year.

Industry

Mining and manufacturing are very important in West Virginia. Together they account for about one-fifth of the state's economy. These two industries have made significant contributions to West Virginia's history as well as its economy.

Industries in West Virginia
Value of Goods and Services in Millions of Dollars

Although mining and manufacturing are major industries, in recent decades many types of service industries have become increasingly important in West Virginia. They include stores, hospitals, banks, restaurants, and government agencies that provide services to people. How would a pie chart showing West Virginia's economy in the 1800s look different from today's chart?

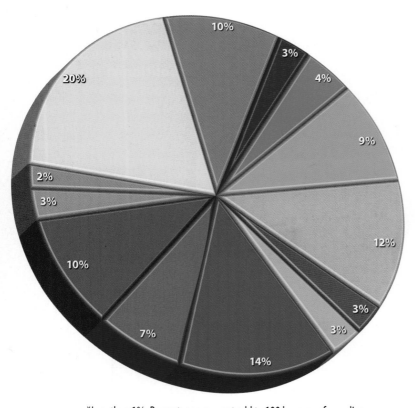

LEGEND

*	Agriculture, Forestry, and Fishing	$204
▦	Mining	$5,985
▪	Utilities	$1,916
▪	Construction	$2,562
▪	Manufacturing	$5,577
▪	Wholesale and Retail Trade	$7,177
▪	Transportation	$1,867
▪	Media and Entertainment	$1,838
▪	Finance, Insurance, and Real Estate	$8,991
▪	Professional and Technical Services	$4,302
*	Education	$305
▪	Health Care	$5,950
▪	Hotels and Restaurants	$1,784
▪	Other Services	$1,450
▪	Government	$12,350
TOTAL		**$62,258**

*Less than 1%. Percentages may not add to 100 because of rounding.

In 2009, West Virginia ranked second, after Wyoming, as the state that mined the most coal. That year, the state's mines produced more than 144 million tons of coal. There are coal deposits in 53 of West Virginia's 55 counties.

West Virginia also mines limestone. The limestone bedrock **quarried** in the state is rich in calcium carbonate, potassium, and phosphorus. The minerals in West Virginia lime make it an excellent fertilizer for farm pastures and lawns. Lime is also used for the production of steel.

Manufacturing areas in West Virginia are along the Kanawha River and the Ohio River, as well as in the cities of Charleston, Huntington, and Wheeling. These areas are responsible for the production of chemicals, glass, **fabricated metals**, high-technology products, and machinery. Some manufacturing in West Virginia makes use of the state's mineral resources as raw materials.

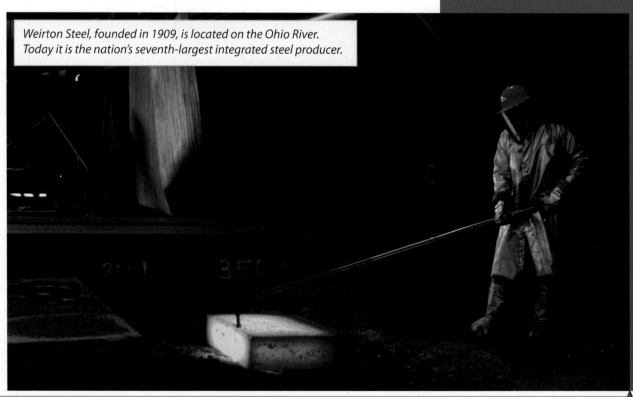

Weirton Steel, founded in 1909, is located on the Ohio River. Today it is the nation's seventh-largest integrated steel producer.

Goods and Services

Large fruit orchards in West Virginia's Eastern Panhandle grow apples and peaches. West Virginia does not have very much flat land for crops, but hay, wheat, oats, soybeans, corn, and tobacco are grown. Farmers also produce dairy products, and they raise **broiler chickens**, turkeys, and cattle.

West Virginia supports more than 23,000 farms. The average farm is less than 200 acres.

West Virginia even has a small wine industry. The southern and central highland valleys grow wonderful wine-making grapes such as Concord, Niagara, and French **hybrids** called Seyval, Foch, and Vidal Blanc. Until the mid-1980s, wine-making was done only on a very small scale. Now the West Virginia government allows the sale of wines produced on large farms.

West Virginia's glass country can be found in the rolling hills of the Tri-State region, where Ohio, Kentucky, and West Virginia meet. Dozens of companies make beautiful glass products using the state's sand deposits. Many **artisans** in this region make handmade and blown glassware and offer glassmaking demonstrations to visitors.

Many West Virginia workers have jobs in the service sector. Some of these jobs are with the government, in health-care facilities, and in public transit. Tourism is an important part of the service industry in West Virginia. More than 65,000 West Virginians are employed in the tourist industry. Some of these people work in restaurants, in hotels, and at tourist attractions.

Decorative glass objects have been handcrafted in parts of West Virginia for more than 100 years.

American Indians

The first people in West Virginia were prehistoric American Indians. These early hunters lived in the area between 8,000 and 10,000 years ago. **Archaeologists** have found their stone tools in the Kanawha and Ohio valleys. These prehistoric people were often on the move and never settled permanently in the area.

Later, several different cultures settled in West Virginia's Northern and Eastern Panhandles. There, archaeologists have uncovered tools, pottery, and ceremonial burial grounds. Most of these remains are from the Adena and Hopewell cultures. The people built large ceremonial mounds, for which they earned the name Mound Builders.

The Grave Creek Mound was a massive undertaking. The Adena had to move nearly 60,000 tons of earth in basket loads. The Hopewell built similar mounds in the Ohio Valley.

The Grave Creek Mound, in Marshall County, is the largest mound in the United States. It is 62 feet high and 240 feet in diameter. Archaeologists believe that it was built between 250 and 150 BC.

By the 1600s, the Lenape, or Delaware, and the Shawnee had moved into West Virginia. At about the same time, the Iroquois Confederacy began coming to the area. The Iroquois Confederacy was an **alliance** of five Iroquois-speaking nations. They are the Mohawk, Oneida, Onondaga, Cayuga, and Seneca groups. In 1722, the Tuscarora joined the Iroquois Confederacy, and it became known as the Six Nations.

European exploration and settlement forced many American Indians west. As a result of this forced migration, there was much tension and bloodshed in the 1600s and 1700s. By the mid-1700s, the Iroquois began to give up their land claims in West Virginia through a series of **treaties**.

In 1777, a frontiersman named Samuel McColloch jumped on horseback into Wheeling Creek to escape from American Indians. He survived and rode off to safety. His amazing leap is a famous tale in West Virginia history.

I DIDN'T KNOW THAT!

Prehistoric American Indians used tools to grind berries, nuts, and plants when preparing food.

The Iroquois Confederacy had a common council, at which chiefs voted on decisions. For most decisions, all the chiefs had to agree.

Many American Indian groups, such as the Shawnee, continued to oppose European settlement until the end of the 1700s.

Chief Logan was a friend to the new settlers but later became a bitter enemy when his family was killed by a group of European men. The city and county of Logan are named for this American Indian.

A European settler discovered Grave Creek Mound in 1770. He fell off the top of it while hunting.

Explorers

I t is thought that the first person of European descent to see what is now West Virginia was John Lederer. Lederer and his group reached the top of the Blue Ridge Mountains, which are along the border between present-day Virginia and West Virginia. At the time, Lederer was exploring for Sir William Berkeley, the governor of the British colony of Virginia. Lederer made a total of three trips to the Blue Ridge Mountains between 1669 and 1670.

The French and the British battled for control of the region for nearly 100 years. The discovery of the New River in 1671 was a turning point for the British. With access to the great river, the British could expand their power by laying claim to the entire Ohio Valley. The expedition that discovered this ancient river was called the Batts and Fallam Expedition. The discovery allowed fur traders and explorers to move farther west, into Virginia's wilderness.

The British eventually defeated the French in the French and Indian War, which lasted from 1754 to 1763. The British then gained complete control over the area that is now West Virginia.

French claims to the West Virginia region were based on the voyages of René-Robert Cavelier, sieur de La Salle. The explorer, born in France in 1643, was also the first European to travel down the Mississippi River to the Gulf of Mexico.

Timeline of Settlement

Colony Established

1607 England establishes the colony of Virginia, with its first settlement at Jamestown.

Early Exploration and Colonization

1669 John Lederer and his companions become the first people of European descent to view what is now West Virginia.

1669 French explorer René-Robert Cavelier, sieur de La Salle, explores the Ohio River.

1671 Thomas Batts and Robert Fallam claim for England land that is now part of West Virginia.

1722 The Iroquois surrender land south of the Ohio River, including areas in the Eastern Panhandle.

1725 Fur traders explore the western Appalachians.

Settlements and Conflict

1731 Morgan Morgan establishes the first settlement in what is now West Virginia, near Bunker Hill.

1732 German, Welsh, Scottish, and Irish pioneers settle in western Virginia.

1783 The American Revolution, which began in 1775, ends in the creation of the United States.

1788 Virginia, including land that is now West Virginia, becomes the 10th state to ratify, or approve, the new U.S. Constitution.

1859 Abolitionist John Brown unsuccessfully raids Harpers Ferry.

Statehood and Civil War

1863 During the Civil War, West Virginia is admitted to the Union as the 35th state, separate from Virginia.

1865 The African American 55th Massachusetts Regiment marches through Charleston. Soon after, the South surrenders, ending the Civil War.

Early Settlers

T he area now known as the Eastern Panhandle attracted West Virginia's early settlers. Colonel Morgan Morgan was one of West Virginia's first settlers. Both Morgantown and Morgan County were named in his family's honor.

Map of Settlements and Resources in Early West Virginia

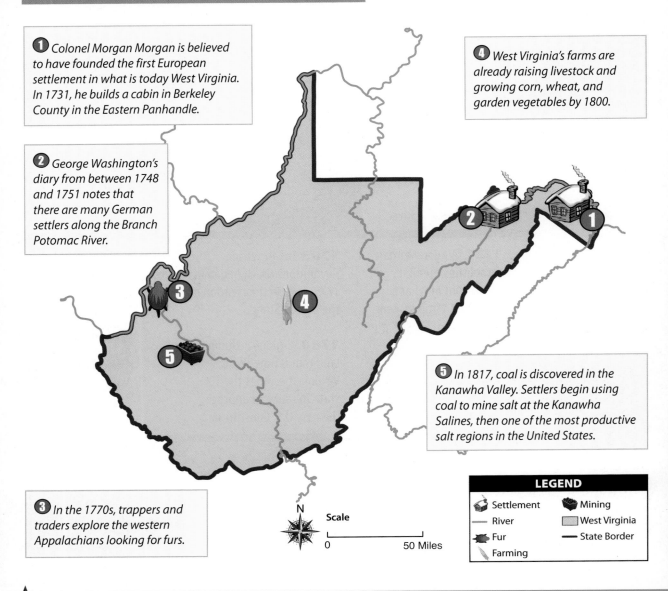

1 Colonel Morgan Morgan is believed to have founded the first European settlement in what is today West Virginia. In 1731, he builds a cabin in Berkeley County in the Eastern Panhandle.

2 George Washington's diary from between 1748 and 1751 notes that there are many German settlers along the Branch Potomac River.

4 West Virginia's farms are already raising livestock and growing corn, wheat, and garden vegetables by 1800.

5 In 1817, coal is discovered in the Kanawha Valley. Settlers begin using coal to mine salt at the Kanawha Salines, then one of the most productive salt regions in the United States.

3 In the 1770s, trappers and traders explore the western Appalachians looking for furs.

N

Scale

0   50 Miles

LEGEND

Settlement		Mining	
River		West Virginia	
Fur		State Border	
Farming			

The Shenandoah Valley was a major southern migration route for Scottish, Irish, and German settlers. Many people from these cultural groups first went to Pennsylvania and New Jersey when they arrived from Europe. Later, they or their descendants moved southwest into what is now West Virginia.

Many settlers built homes along West Virginia's rivers, but a few settled on the Allegheny Plateau. By 1800, West Virginia's population had risen to 78,000. Most West Virginia families at this time made their living by farming. Settlement in the region continued to grow as natural resources, such as coal and oil, were discovered.

Industrialization in the late 1800s and early 1900s encouraged many African Americans to move to West Virginia to find work. Harpers Ferry was notable as a center of 19th century industry.

Notable People

Many notable people from West Virginia have contributed to the development of the 35th state as well as the rest of the country. The residents of West Virginia have historically shown independent spirits. Before and after the region split from Virginia in 1863, the Mountain State has been home to prominent military leaders, educators, scientists, social and political activists, and artists.

CHIEF LOGAN
(c. 1725–1780)

Chief Logan, a Cayuga Indian, lived in the Ohio River Valley. Colonists murdered his family in an attack in 1774. Logan retaliated, helping to start the last war in which colonists fought on the side of Great Britain before the American Revolution. Logan refused to take part in peace negotiations and is remembered for his speech known as "Logan's Lament."

STONEWALL JACKSON
(1824–1863)

Thomas Jonathan "Stonewall" Jackson was born in 1824 in Clarksburg, Virginia, now West Virginia. He did not support slavery. However, when Virginia joined the Confederacy at the beginning of the Civil War, he became a general in the Confederate army. A celebrated commander, Jackson earned his nickname on the battlefields, where he stood "like a stone wall." He died in 1863, shot accidentally by his own men.

BOOKER T. WASHINGTON (1856–1915)

Washington was born a slave in Virginia in 1856. After he was freed, he moved with his family to West Virginia and worked hard to educate himself. Later he headed a school for African Americans in Tuskegee, Alabama. Booker T. Washington, who focused on improving the position of freed slaves in the country, became a powerful political activist.

WALTER REUTHER (1907–1970)

Born in Wheeling, Reuther became a prominent U.S. labor union leader. A factory worker from the age of 16, he helped organize sit-down strikes in the late 1930s. Reuther served as president of the United Automobile Workers, or UAW, from 1946 until his death in 1970.

CHUCK YEAGER (1923–)

Charles "Chuck" Elwood Yeager became the first person to fly faster than the speed of sound. On October 14, 1947, he broke the sound barrier while flying the experimental Bell X-1. He also became the first person to fly at more than twice the speed of sound. Yeager was born at Myra in Lincoln County.

I DIDN'T KNOW THAT!

Nancy Hanks Lincoln (1784–1818), born in what is now West Virginia, was the mother of 16th U.S. president, Abraham Lincoln. When her son was nine years old, she died from drinking contaminated milk. She is a distant relative of Academy Award–winning actor Tom Hanks.

Morgan Spurlock (1970–), born in Parkersburg, is a filmmaker. In his best-known film, *Super Size Me*, he documented his health while eating only fast food for 30 days.

Population

West Virginia is the 37th most populated state in the country. There are more than 1.8 million people living in the state. About 95 percent of West Virginians are of European heritage, while almost 4 percent are African American.

The state has, in recent years, seen little change in population because West Virginia has experienced a low **birthrate**, as well as migration out of the state. West Virginia's average birthrate of about 11 births per 1,000 people is below the national average of 14 per 1,000 people.

West Virginia Population 1950–2010

Unlike many U.S. states, West Virginia has seen an overall decline in its population since 1950. What impact might a drop in population have on the state's government and economy?

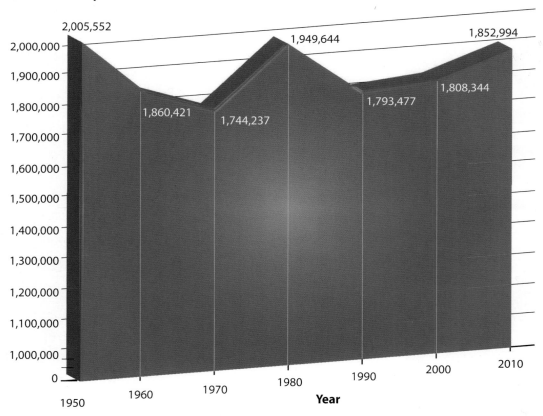

Number of People

- 2,005,552
- 1,949,644
- 1,852,994
- 1,860,421
- 1,744,237
- 1,793,477
- 1,808,344

2,000,000
1,900,000
1,800,000
1,700,000
1,600,000
1,500,000
1,400,000
1,300,000
1,200,000
1,100,000
1,000,000
0

1950 1960 1970 1980 1990 2000 2010

Year

About 27 percent of West Virginia households include one or more members 65 years of age or older.

Established in 1762, Shepherdstown is the oldest town in West Virginia. The town has fewer than 1,000 residents.

Politics and Government

West Virginia's government is divided into three branches. They are the executive, the legislative, and the judicial branches. The executive branch carries out state laws. The legislative branch makes new laws and changes existing ones. The judicial branch enforces and interprets the laws. All of the high-level officeholders in the three branches are elected by the people of West Virginia.

Located in Charleston, West Virginia's limestone and marble state house was opened in 1932.

The executive branch is headed by a governor, who is elected for a four-year term. The governor is responsible for proposing the state budget, for appointing state department directors, and for signing bills into laws. The state's legislature has a Senate with 34 members and a House of Delegates with 100 members. West Virginia adopted three state songs in 1963. "West Virginia Hills" is sung by the people of West Virginia to remember their origin and the remarkable features of their state.

The Supreme Court of Appeals is West Virginia's highest court. It has five judges, who are called justices and who serve 12-year terms. Lower courts in the state include circuit courts and magistrate courts.

West Virginia's state legislature meets inside the state house. The office of the governor is also located in this building.

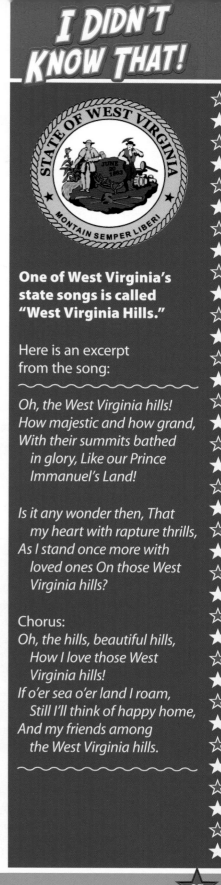

One of West Virginia's state songs is called "West Virginia Hills."

Here is an excerpt from the song:

Oh, the West Virginia hills!
How majestic and how grand,
With their summits bathed
in glory, Like our Prince
Immanuel's Land!

Is it any wonder then, That
my heart with rapture thrills,
As I stand once more with
loved ones On those West
Virginia hills?

Chorus:
Oh, the hills, beautiful hills,
How I love those West
Virginia hills!
If o'er sea o'er land I roam,
Still I'll think of happy home,
And my friends among
the West Virginia hills.

Cultural Groups

Until the 1890s people of German and Scots-Irish heritage were the most numerous ethnic groups. At that time the industrial expansion of the state attracted many European immigrants. Today about 1 percent of the people of West Virginia are foreign-born. Many of West Virginia's farm families are descended from early settlers and have owned their land for generations.

Deep in the heart of the Potomac Valley's Randolph County is a small community established by Swiss immigrants. They named their town Helvetia in honor of their homeland. *Helvetia* is the word for "Switzerland" in Latin. Many of the town's buildings were modeled after the architecture of Switzerland, and a Swiss-German **dialect** can still be heard in the streets.

Each October, the Mountain State Forest Festival in Elkins offers a country music show, arts and crafts, a lumberjack contest, and three parades.

A dulcimer is a stringed folk instrument that is held on the lap and played by plucking or strumming.

The city of Elkins hosts one of West Virginia's oldest and largest festivals. The Mountain State Forest Festival celebrates the important role that natural resources play in the state's economic development.

West Virginia recognizes and celebrates the cultural heritage of the state's coal-mining industry. Since coal was discovered in southern West Virginia in 1742 along the Coal River, more than 4 billion tons have been mined from these historic coalfields.

In the town of Augusta, the Augusta Heritage Center teaches old-time banjo playing. The banjo is a popular traditional folk instrument in West Virginia. The Vandalia Gathering in Charleston honors the state's ethnic heritage. Irish, Swiss, Scottish, and Appalachian styles of dance take place. Banjo, guitar, and dulcimer musicians compete for prizes.

I DIDN'T KNOW THAT!

Historic Shepherdstown is host to the Appalachian Heritage Festival.

Charles Town, in the Shenandoah Valley, was named in honor of George Washington's youngest brother, Charles. He gave many acres of land to the growing village.

Clarksburg celebrates the Italian Heritage Festival in September. The three-day festival attracts more than 150,000 visitors.

The legend of John Henry, "the steel drivin' man," comes from the construction of a rail tunnel near Talcott in southern West Virginia. Storytellers say that John could hammer like no one else and that he was even faster than a hammer drill machine.

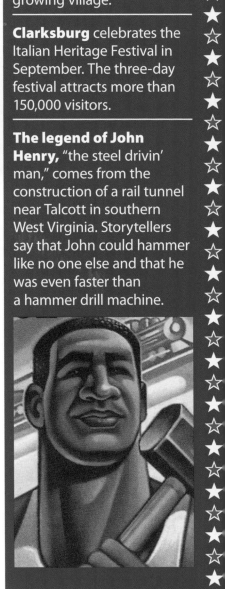

Arts and Entertainment

There has always been a love of bluegrass and country music in West Virginia. The music capital of the state is Wheeling, where the live-radio country music show *Jamboree USA* is broadcast to devoted listeners. It is the second-oldest live radio show in the United States.

West Virginia's strong country music roots has produced many singing stars. Grammy-winning Kathy Mattea has recorded more than a dozen studio albums and has enjoyed enormous fan support, along with many number-one hits.

One of West Virginia's most famous writers is Pearl S. Buck, who won the Pulitzer Prize in 1932 for her book *The Good Earth*. Buck also won the Nobel Prize for Literature. She is the only woman from the United States to win both awards. She was born and raised in Hillsboro, which is part of West Virginia's Pocahontas County.

In 1938, Pearl S. Buck became the third American to win the Nobel Prize for Literature. The first two winners from the United States were novelist Sinclair Lewis, in 1930, and playwright Eugene O'Neill, in 1936.

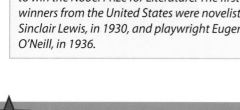

In June, the Greenbrier Valley Festival of the Arts is held in Lewisburg. Local artists and musicians gather to present a weekend of world-class entertainment. The Eastern Panhandle is very proud of its history. Each spring the region celebrates the past with large festivals, such as the Mountain Heritage Arts and Crafts Festival. Many of the most important playwrights from the United States are showcased at the month-long Contemporary American Theater Festival at Shepherd College in Shepherdstown.

Jennifer Garner grew up in West Virginia. She is perhaps best-known for her role in the television series *Alias*. She went on to appear in several films, including *The Invention of Lying* in 2009. She is married to actor and director Ben Affleck.

Jennifer Garner, raised in Charleston, has starred in many successful movies, including 13 Going on 30.

Sports

Race-car driving in the Shenandoah Valley is very popular, even with movie stars. Both Paul Newman and Tom Cruise paid regular visits to West Virginia's Summit Point Raceway. It is considered one of the most challenging auto racing tracks in the nation. The raceway hosts Sports Car Club of America events for professional and amateur auto racing, as well as motorcycle and go-cart races.

Summit Point Raceway features a 2-mile course. It also offers lessons in accident avoidance, police driving, and security driving.

West Virginia is home to a number of popular yet unusual sports. Rock climbers from around the nation come to the Potomac Highlands to climb the incredible sandstone formations known as the Seneca Rocks. Wood chopping is another unusual sport that is practiced in West Virginia. A back-breaking competition is held yearly at the Webster County Woodchopping Festival. The rugged and difficult life of the lumberjack is celebrated by competitors from around the world.

West Virginia has excellent white-water rafting along some of its wilder rivers. Sometimes called the Grand Canyon of the East, the New River Gorge National Park is a popular tourist attraction. In the Gauley River National Recreational Area there are some difficult rapids, whose names include "Heaven Help You" and "Lost Paddle."

White-water rafting brings thousands of thrill seekers to West Virginia waters.

National Averages Comparison

The United States is a federal republic, consisting of fifty states and the District of Columbia. Alaska and Hawai'i are the only non-contiguous, or non-touching, states in the nation. Today, the United States of America is the third-largest country in the world in population. The United States Census Bureau takes a census, or count of all the people, every ten years. It also regularly collects other kinds of data about the population and the economy. How does West Virginia compare with the national average?

Comparison Chart

United States 2010 Census Data *	USA	West Virginia
Admission to Union	NA	June 20, 1863
Land Area (in square miles)	3,537,438.44	24,077.73
Population Total	308,745,538	1,852,994
Population Density (people per square mile)	87.28	76.96
Population Percentage Change (April 1, 2000, to April 1, 2010)	9.7%	2.5%
White Persons (percent)	72.4%	93.9%
Black Persons (percent)	12.6%	3.4%
American Indian and Alaska Native Persons (percent)	0.9%	0.2%
Asian Persons (percent)	4.8%	0.7%
Native Hawaiian and Other Pacific Islander Persons (percent)	0.2%	—
Some Other Race (percent)	6.2%	0.3%
Persons Reporting Two or More Races (percent)	2.9%	1.5%
Persons of Hispanic or Latino Origin (percent)	16.3%	1.2%
Not of Hispanic or Latino Origin (percent)	83.7%	98.8%
Median Household Income	$52,029	$37,528
Percentage of People Age 25 or Over Who Have Graduated from High School	80.4%	75.2%

*All figures are based on the 2010 United States Census, with the exception of the last two items.

How to Improve My Community

Strong communities make strong states. Think about what features are important in your community. What do you value? Education? Health? Forests? Safety? Beautiful spaces? Government works to help citizens create ideal living conditions that are fair to all by providing services in communities. Consider what changes you could make in your community. How would they improve your state as a whole? Using this concept web as a guide, write a report that outlines the features you think are most important in your community and what improvements could be made. A strong state needs strong communities.

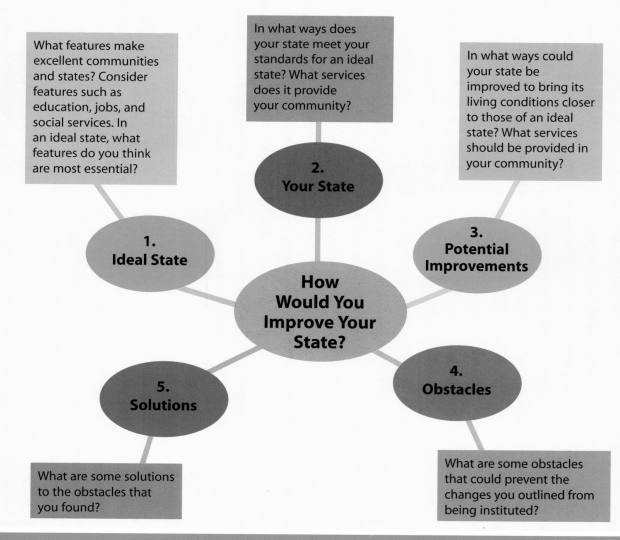

What features make excellent communities and states? Consider features such as education, jobs, and social services. In an ideal state, what features do you think are most essential?

In what ways does your state meet your standards for an ideal state? What services does it provide your community?

In what ways could your state be improved to bring its living conditions closer to those of an ideal state? What services should be provided in your community?

2. Your State

1. Ideal State

3. Potential Improvements

How Would You Improve Your State?

5. Solutions

4. Obstacles

What are some solutions to the obstacles that you found?

What are some obstacles that could prevent the changes you outlined from being instituted?

Exercise Your Mind!

Think about these questions and then use your research skills to find the answers and learn more fascinating facts about West Virginia. A teacher, librarian, or parent may be able to help you locate the best sources to use in your research.

1 *Shenandoah* is an American Indian word that means:

a. "Daughter of the Mountains"
b. "Daughter of the Valley"
c. "Daughter of the Stars"
d. "Daughter of Denver"

2 What kind of apple is the state fruit of West Virginia?

3 Which city in West Virginia is known as the Nail City?

4 What is the town of Grafton known for?

5 Which family feud started over a pig?

6 Who launched a steamboat long before Robert Fulton did?

7 Who was Punch Jones?

8 Harpers Ferry National Historical Park is located in which area of West Virginia?

a. Ohio River Valley
b. Potomac Highlands
c. Eastern Panhandle
d. Shenandoah Valley

Words to Know

abolitionist: someone who wants to put an end to slavery

alliance: a union

archaeologists: scientists who study early peoples through artifacts and remains

artisans: highly skilled craftspeople

birthrate: the number of births compared to the total population

bituminous coal: a type of soft coal that burns with a smoky flame

broiler chickens: chickens raised for their meat rather than their eggs

dialect: a particular variety of a language, usually specific to a geographic area

fabricated metals: metals that are manufactured, such as steel

hybrids: combinations of two different plants

median age: in population, the age at which exactly half of the population is older and the other half is younger

migratory: moving from one place to another

quarried: removed as a stone from an excavation pit

rural: relating to the countryside, people who live in the country, or agriculture

sediment: minerals and organic matter that are deposited by water or ice

spa: a resort people go to in order to benefit from the site's mineral-rich waters

treaties: formal agreements between two parties

venomous: containing or producing a poison called venom

Index

Log on to www.av2books.com

AV² by Weigl brings you media enhanced books that support active learning. Go to www.av2books.com, and enter the special code found on page 2 of this book. You will gain access to enriched and enhanced content that supplements and complements this book. Content includes video, audio, web links, quizzes, a slide show, and activities.

Audio
Listen to sections of the book read aloud.

Video
Watch informative video clips.

Embedded Weblinks
Gain additional information for research.

Try This!
Complete activities and hands-on experiments.

WHAT'S ONLINE?

Try This!	**Embedded Weblinks**	**Video**	**EXTRA FEATURES**
Test your knowledge of the state in a mapping activity.	Discover more attractions in West Virginia.	Watch a video introduction to West Virginia..	**Audio** Listen to sections of the book read aloud.
Find out more about precipitation in your city.	Learn more about the history of the state.	Watch a video about the features of the state.	
Plan what attractions you would like to visit in the state.	Learn the full lyrics of the state song.		**Key Words** Study vocabulary, and complete a matching word activity.
Learn more about the early natural resources of the state.			
Write a biography about a notable resident of West Virginia.			**Slide Show** View images and captions, and prepare a presentation.
Complete an educational census activity.			**Quizzes** Test your knowledge.

AV² was built to bridge the gap between print and digital. We encourage you to tell us what you like and what you want to see in the future.

Sign up to be an AV² Ambassador at www.av2books.com/ambassador.